From the Heart

Linda Cotton

Copyright © 2014 Linda Cotton

All rights reserved. No part of this book may be used or reproduced by any means, graphic, electronic, or mechanical, including photocopying, recording, taping or by any information storage retrieval system without the written permission of the publisher except in the case of brief quotations embodied in critical articles and reviews.

Serenity Press Publishing books may be ordered through booksellers or by contacting:

Serenity Press Publishing
www.serenitypress.org
serenitypress@hotmail.com

Because of the dynamic nature of the Internet, any web addresses or links contained in this book may have changed since publication and may no longer be valid. The views expressed in this work are solely those of the author and do not necessarily reflect the views of the publisher and the publisher hereby disclaims any responsibility for them.

The author of this book does not dispense medical advice or prescribe the use of any technique as a form of treatment for physical, emotional, or medical problems without the advice of a physician, either directly or indirectly. The intent of the author is only to offer information of a general nature to help you in your quest for emotional and spiritual well-being. In the event you use any of the information in this book for yourself, which is your constitutional right, the author and the publisher assume no responsibility for your actions.

ISBN: (sc) 978-0-9925231-5-2
ISBN: (e)   978-0-9925231-6-9

Table of Contents

Dedication	1
My Childhood	3
Valentine's Day	6
Marriage	7
Our Special Mum	10
Our Special Dad	11
Letter from John	12
John	13
John for Your Farewell	14
My One and Only J C	15
Time	17
Our Lovely Tony	18
Our Lovely Terry	19
Life Must Go On	20
When	22
My Son's Wedding Day	23
The Dawning of 2006	24
Cycling Sunday Morning	26
Fossie, Sandi & Kids	28

Our Precious Danny	29
My Daughter's Wedding Blessing	32
Australia Day 2007	34
Morning after Australia Day 2007	36
Our Lovely Children	38
Travellers	40
An Ode to the Searles	41
Karen – My True Friend	43
Me – The Rose Bush	44
Reflections	45
A Home called "Alderney"	46
Down to the Glen	48
Tripping Round Australia	49
Saturday Morning Cycle Along the Bay	50
Sunday Morning Swing	52
Along the Bay	54
Flying High over Warnbro Sound	55
Sunday Morn on the Patio	56
My Best Friend	57
Sisters' Saturday Morning Cycle	58
The Garden of Love	60

Our Lovely Pam	62
Naburn Farm	64
Walking and Reminiscing	65
A Dear Friend	71
May Storm	73
My Lovely Sister's Special Birthday	75
Star Gazing	77
"Calma" The Dolphin	78
Farewell to My Lovely Grandsons	79
First day of Winter	81
From my Patio	83
Farewell to My Lovely Grandchildren	85
J C's Birthday 2014	86
Mother's Day	87
About the Author	89
Testimonials	91

Dedication

I would like to dedicate this book to my John (JC),
our wonderful son Glenn and beautiful daughter
Nadina (Dina).

The love we all share cannot be measured, but enjoyed.
True love lasts forever.

Our children are amazing, always showing such love,
strength and caring, but even more through such
devastating times. We may be miles apart, but love
truly shortens the distance.

Me x

My Childhood

When I was a child
Not much money was around
But the love in our house
Truly did abound

There were four children
In our family
I was the youngest
Two brothers, a sister and me

Mum and Dad brought us up
Doing the best they could
Both working very hard
Supplying a home and food

Dad worked on the aircraft
Cycling every day
Over the years did many miles
Just to bring home his pay

Mum had many part-time jobs
But loved to be at home
Bringing up us children
While Dad cycled along

We were all so active
And all loved our sport
Spending many times together
With good manners being taught

Our early holidays we spent
With cases packed, just right
Travelling on buses, trains and ferries
Across to the *Isle of Wight*

What wonderful memories
We made over these years
How Mum and Dad managed
Would bring you to tears

Our chalet was called 'Happy Days'
And it certainly was true
As we sat in the garden
Over the sea, what a view

When the boys were old enough
They joined the 'Boys Brigade'
Both becoming drummers
Marching in the local parade

My sister and I joined netball teams
And played many matches too
Winning, brought smiles and beams
Making us feel good it's true

When I was ten, our youngest brother came along
Bringing more happiness to us all
And soon after, the elder three
Got married, starting families, I recall

He was a very clever child
And had so much energy
Often driving our parents wild
But a treasure he came to be

He loved to play the piano
And really did work hard
Practicing his scales and tunes
We could hear him from the yard

We all became so very close
And spent many a lovely time
Out for the day in a car
With my future husband, so sublime

My siblings all did the same
Taking us out for the day
And there were many family parties
Over the years, along the way

So my childhood was just special
Great memories to treasure
And all the love our parents shared
Brought our family so much pleasure

Me x

Valentine's Day

It's wonderful to know you
I think you're really grand
Many words I find so hard to express
I hope you'll understand

But darling you know I love you
In everything you do
So will you be my Valentine
Today and all life through

Me x

(First poem to John for Valentine's Day Feb 1965)

Marriage

When John and I married
It was such a happy day
Memories to treasure
But we soon travelled away

To start a new life
Miles across the sea
It was an adventure
For my 'new husband' and me

We spent a few years
Doing things that were new
In bright sunny Africa
Cooking on the BBQ

We worked very hard
To save money it was true
Spending time with my brother
And his young family too

We travelled the country
Visiting National Parks too
Seeing the mountains
Rise out of the blue

The sights were amazing
Nothing could compare
The beautiful sun rise
Peace everywhere

We started our family
Our baby son was born
Then another on the way
We felt it time to go home

My brother and family
And all of us too
Had a wonderful camping trip
Down the coast, to join a ship's crew

The ship carried us back
To our homeland 'cross the sea
Oh what an adventure
For my family and me

We all settled back home
For a number of years
Our daughter was born
Bringing such happy tears

Oh what happiness
Our children did bring
We loved our family unit
Such a precious thing

Me x

Our Special Mum

Dear Mum you now are laid to rest
With no more pain to bear
We're sending all our love to you
To show that we all care

You brought us love and laughter
With every day that passed
We have such happy memories
Which in our hearts will last

Your thoughtfulness and kindness
To us, and many others
Will always stay within our hearts
- You were the best of Mothers

You taught us all such loving ways
And hope these will remain
Within ourselves, and families
Until we meet again

Me x

(Poem for our Mum when she died Jan 1991)

Our Special Dad

Dear Dad this is the moment
You have been waiting for
With you and Mum together
Just as you were before

You lived your life for all of us
And we hope that we can say
We gave you years of happiness
- Until your dying day

We thank you for your thoughtfulness
And all the things you've done
You sacrificed so many things
To make our house a home

So take our love to keep with you
And just enjoy your sleep
And in our hearts we'll always have
  -   Great memories to keep

Me x

(Poem for our Dad, died January 1991 with Mum)

Letter from John

> 1991 is a year we will always remember, for all the wrong reasons.
>
> Pains might not completely go away, but they will ease with time. Your love & caring for others will always means that you will have friends.
>
> Stay happy, when your happy, I'm happy, and with you by my side there is nothing we cannot overcome.
>
> All my love forever
>
> J.C. xxxx

(John's letter to me after losing my parents)

John

Our hearts, our lives, are broken now
And feel will never mend
But through your love for all of us
- Comes strength to carry on

The sun and moon will always shine
And truly light our way
But we know it's really you
To guide us every day

We all enjoyed such simple things
Which gave us so much pleasure
So in our hearts we'll always have
Your love – to always treasure

So bye for now
And feel no pain
Until we are
- Just one again

Me x

(Poem I wrote and read at my Hubby's funeral 1993)

John for Your Farewell

This time is truly difficult
For me to comprehend
We spent our lives together
My lover, my best friend

The many things we all enjoyed
Cannot be taken, or destroyed
As these are memories we shared
- Knowing that we always cared

'In sickness and in health' – the vow
We carried out, and yet somehow
It doesn't seem so fair to me
To have you taken – suddenly

You did no wrong, you gave your all
And we could ask no more
You brought such love and laughter
- To everybody's door

So we will just say 'bye' for now
And hope you feel no pain
Until we are together
- And all as one again
Me x

(I wrote and read at the Chapel for my Hubby)

My One and Only J C

The time has come for me to let
A part of you set sail, and yet
Together we will always be
As I spread your ashes on the sea

You loved New Zealand so much, I know
And it's hard for me to let you go,
But I am with you every day
And in my heart you'll always stay

Glenn & Dina are with us too
- In their hearts as one, with you
The love that we all shared together
Will always last with us, forever

Margaret, Dick & big Glenn too
Are sharing this moment to be with you
Such friendships that cannot be measured
With them, will be forever treasured

Friends, relations are with you now
In spirit not body, and yet somehow
They find it hard to let you go
As you were loved by many, I know

It's not goodbye that is so strong
Just a small part, where you belong
Our love goes with you, out to sea
So you may rest, where you loved to be

Me x

(Scattering John's ashes on a bay in NZ)

Time

Time is what you give us
Whether near or far apart
So we're sending all our love to you
Which comes right from the heart

In happy times and sad ones too
We've been there for each other
So we would like to thank you
Our special Uncle and great Brother

Mum and Dad would be so proud
To see what you've achieved
And I know that you are grateful
For in you, they believed

Endless love and heartfelt trust
We all give to one another
And this will see us through our lives
And keep our hearts together
Love Us

Linda, Glenn, Dina xxx

(For my brother Fossie's 40th Birthday)

Our Lovely Tony

Today we are all gathered here
As one big family
To guide our lovely Tony -
On a road so heavenly

He always lived life to the full
Had hobbies by the score
Photography - terr-ar-iums
I could mention many more

He loved to play his guitar
- And his singing wasn't bad !!
And o'er the years I know there were -
Good sing-songs to be had

So Tony will not leave us
We will not be apart
As we have such good memories
To keep within our heart

Me x

(For my lovely Brother-in-Law Aug 1999)

Our Lovely Terry

As I sit looking out to sea
Memories of Terry flood back to me
Always so tidy in all he would do
So loving, so caring, thinking of others it's true

He loved to laugh and chuckle too
Loved tinkling with bikes, to make them look new
He loved to take photos - and take his time -
To make them the best - oh that one's fine!

So together we're gathered to send all our love
To Terry, so special, on his journey above
Husband, Dad, Brother, - Uncle, Grandad too
"We all love you dearly - and will miss you"

But deep in our hearts
That's where Terry will stay
Till we all meet again
- On our chosen day

Me x

(For my eldest Brother Terry in Canada June 2000)

Life Must Go On

People say – "Life must go on"
But don't know how it feels
To have the one you truly love
Just removed like a damaged wheel

It's like a wave from head to toe
That takes your breath away and so
The feeling that it leaves behind
You have to deal with, in your mind

You don't know why you carry on
The reasons left, they have all gone
But after many tears and sighs
Something makes you realise

You have a life and family
To make the most of and agree
To give up now would be a sin
A new life now – just must begin

The years that have now passed before
Will stay with me for ever more
The truly happy times we shared
I'll always know you really cared

Those memories are treasured now
So give me strength, and show me how
To carry on and see me through
Till I am once again with you

Me x

(My thoughts months after losing JC)

When

When you walk with me I feel as proud as can be
When you talk with me it feels like butterflies are in me
When you touch me I'm sure I am dreaming
My face must show it, as it is definitely gleaming

When it comes down to it, all I think of is you
Wish we could be stuck together with a little bit of glue
Can't believe we met so far away
I want to be with you forever and a day

Me x

(From my son Glenn to his Fiancée)

My Son's Wedding Day

Today is such a special day
When two hearts become one
Three and more years have gone by
Since Vicki met my Son

I was so happy from the start
That they were together
And I know that this bond
Will last until forever

So join me now to toast their health
And for those who can't be here
To wish them love and happiness
For each and every year

All my love forever
x Mum x

(Poem I wrote and read at my Son Glenn and Daughter-in-Law Vicki's wedding in 2003)

The Dawning of 2006

Another year is dawning
I wonder what's in store
I hope everyone's works out
Better than the one before

Health and happiness I wish
For friends and family
And to hope this world could live
In peace and harmony

There are so many lovely things
That happen every day
We don't need hate and violence
To help us on our way

If people stopped, just for a while
To see the simple things of life
They'd all enjoy the pleasures
Without daily stress and strife

"Stop and smell the roses"
Is a saying we've all heard
And if you take notice –
There is truth in every word

People have to go to work
And bring up families
But everyone could take the time
To make treasured memories

So give yourself the time you need
To reflect on lovely things
And I know you'll truly feel
The peace inside it brings

So I hope this New Year
Has doors that open wide
But even more importantly
You're happy with yourself inside

Me x

Cycling Sunday Morning

It is Sunday morning
I've been out for a ride
I've been feeling very sad
I want you by my side
Enjoying this lovely life style
So free, with not a care
But you are always in my heart
And with me everywhere

But you are missing
What we came here for
The freedom, the space,
Just being by the shore
Today is your Birthday
I cannot celebrate
Because you have been taken
To that "Pearly Gate"

So many things happening
The kids in the UK
And I'm just sitting here alone
Overlooking the bay
It is so beautiful
Just being here
Wish we were all together
But in our hearts we're near

I know I have to
"Get on with life"
But I always treasured
Just being your wife
And being a mother
Of our special two
But I have that knowledge
That they're a part of you

Thank you for the wonderful years
Together, that we had
You were a marvellous husband
And a truly great Dad
We all really miss you
But in our hearts you'll stay
Till we all meet again
On some other day

Me x

(John's Birthday 23 April 2006)

Fossie, Sandi & Kids

The time has come for you to go
And I'm not full of cheer
It has been so lovely
Having you so near

I know it's been a short while
But the memories I will treasure
Just being all together here
Has given me such pleasure

Thank you for just everything
And the time we spent together
And I know my love for you
Will last until forever

Luv always
Me x

(My brother and his family returning to the UK, after holiday - 2006)

Our Precious Danny

Our precious Danny
Lies here today
In Manchester United kit
Playing – 'home or away'

He was loved by so many
Family, friends, children and wife
He was so vibrant
- And just enjoyed life

Not one for the kitchen
- He kept out of there!
Nor one for the garden
Except playing – without a care

When he was younger
John tried, but in vain
To teach our dear Fossie
To get a car started again!

He was too busy
Kicking a ball in the air
To take any notice
About cars – not a care!

He learnt the piano
T'was music to our ears
Putting in so much effort
What a pleasure o'er the years

He'd always be there
Any time of the day
If you had a problem
Needing help in some way

He was so loving
- Reliable too
He would do anything
Making things better for you

On a personal side
He was there for us three
In our tender moments
Even far across the sea

His own precious family
Son, daughter and wife
He treasured the years
Which completed his life

Not always on time!
I know you'll agree
"Hold up that meeting
- It can't start without me!"

So let us all think
Of those years full of pleasure
Spent with our lovely Danny
Wonderful memories to treasure

He is joining our family
And friends high above
I know there'll be laughter
Tears, and lots of love

He won't be cold
Crocheted blankets and a hat
I know that is true
- Our Mum will see to that!

This is not goodbye
We'll never be apart
For our precious Danny
Is forever in our heart

Forever
Me x

(My eulogy I wrote & read for youngest brother Danny's (Fossie) passing)

My Daughter's Wedding Blessing

From Seychelles to the UK
They have travelled in their life
To take their vows and celebrate
To become 'Husband and Wife'

We are all gathered here
On this Blessing Day
To celebrate this happy time
And dance the night away

I am truly happy
And sure that you are too
That we are all together
To hear them say "I do"

This is such a special day
For everyone, far and near
And truly lovely memories
Will be treasured and held so dear

I am sure you will all join me
As these precious words I say
"From this day forth may life be good
With health and happiness every day"

All my love forever
x Mum x

(Poem I wrote and read at my Daughter Dina and Son-in-Law Phil's Blessing in UK, after their wedding in the Seychelles in 2006)

Australia Day 2007

Sitting out here
On Australia Day
The sun has gone down
The light drifting away

But the lights in the sky
Are the fireworks' glow
People celebrating the day
In the way that they know

The beaches are full
Of people having fun
Families getting together
The night's just begun

The temperature soared
To 41 degrees
All we could do
Was swim in the seas

The wind's coming up
But it really is warm
And because it's so hot
We are in for a storm

The skies are so pretty
Coloured lights everywhere
Oh that's another firework
Sparkling over there

This is the end
Of a perfect day
Sitting on the patio
Overlooking the Bay

Me x

Morning after Australia Day 2007

The morning after
Forty-one degrees
The wind is blowing
Through the trees

The sun is trying
To peak through
The cluster of clouds
Some grey, some blue

The sea is grey,
With waves of white
Oh what a difference
Just over night

From the heat of the day
And boiling sand
To the cool of this morning
Over the land

It is so peaceful
Looking out to sea
With a motorboat pulling
Someone learning to ski

Three small 'planes
Flying up high
Now doing acrobats
And circles in the sky

Oh what a lovely
Feeling that must be
As free as a bird
Flying high o'er the sea

The show is now over
The 'planes have flown away
But oh what a lovely sight
For the start of the day

The wind is now easing
The trees gently sway
Blue skies now appearing
Perhaps another hot day

Me x

Our Lovely Children

We have two lovely children
And we spent such happy days
Just all being together
In so many different ways

When they were small, we'd go for walks
Down the lane, across the farm
And later playing hide and seek
Having picnics on the lawn

Our holidays spent camping
We all had so much fun
And sleeping well under the stars
When the busy day was done

We all became so very close
With love just all around
And life was full of happiness
And great memories did abound

They both enjoyed their sporting days
And we all spent many a day
In the garden playing tennis
Till the sun had gone away

Growing up they both had
Their own personalities it's true
But the love they shared between them
Was so strong and even grew

Now they are both so happy
Married, with their own families
Enjoying their partners and children
Making treasured memories

Me x

Travellers

Today is such a special day
For these travellers three
From scratch the work has been done
From inside this big combi

We hope your journey will be fun
From the day you leave us here
Good luck be with you and take care
Till we see you again next year

Me x

(My friends and I refitting Combi for their Australian trip)

An Ode to the Searles

The end of an era
Has come to us all
But over the years
We've all had a ball

A family – so special
Over a great many years
Has been through so many things
Through laughter and tears

Parties and weddings –
And some sad days too
We've all helped each other
To see us all through

We have such good memories
To last all our days
And hopefully pass them on
In our great family ways

Love is a special thing
We have for each other
And this was all passed
From our Father and Mother

So treasure our memories
Enjoy life while we may
Know our love for each other
Will last forever and a day

Me x

(For my Mother's family, as we lost the last one)

Karen – My True Friend

Today is such a special day
Your Birthday's come around
I am so glad that I can say
Again our friendship has been found
Years have gone without a word
Between us that is true
But I have always felt inside
I'd find my friend again, that's you

So on this day I hope you can
Celebrate in style
And know that deep in my heart
I will always wear a smile
To know that we can keep in touch
Though miles keep us apart
But friendships grow – near or far
And are kept within the heart.

Me x

(Reuniting after years of lost contact)

Me – The Rose Bush

Me, as a rose bush
Standing there
You, in your other world
Love everywhere

Beautiful petals
All spread out
You in the garden
Love all about

I feel I can grow
With you in my heart
I know that deep down
We'll never part

But I will be stronger
And grow ever more
As you give me strength
To just 'close that door'

Me x

(From a group meeting to *Close the Door* and *Reflect* on grief)

Reflections

My life has been so full of love
And this will help me through
This awful time of loneliness
Now I am not with you

My love for you will never die
And in my heart you'll stay
And give me strength to carry on
With each and every day

I thank you for the wondrous years
That we spent together
And these will give me strength I know
From now – until forever
Me x

(From a group meeting to *Close the Door* and *Reflect* on grief)

A Home called "Alderney"

From the time I walked in
I could feel such a glow
A lovely warm feeling
In me, started to grow

A chat in the kitchen
A quick glance around
Then out in the garden
To see the spa, below ground

Sitting round a small table
We were handed a drink
Nibbling biscuits, homemade pate
Charged our glasses with a chink

Just a small get together
What a friendly affair
It was so pleasant
Shimmering lights everywhere

There was much chatter
And laughter to be heard
And high in the trees
The chirping of a bird

There were snags on the barbie
Salads and chips on display
We all had a good feast
At the end of the day

Then a tour of the house
Which I could not believe
The warmth and the history
This lovely home did just weave

The colours, the woodwork
The old-fashioned design
The lovely old artifacts
Great pieces built through time

There is only one word
That describes it for me
This home full of character
- And that's "ALDERNEY"

Me x

(Visiting friends' renovated home)

Down to the Glen

The peaceful hills surround us
And shades of green abound
The birds are chirping loudly
As they fly all around

The deafening sound of silence
Is so calming for the mind
No noisy sound of industry
- No bustling traffic found

This place just seems like heaven
- A pleasure to behold
The blossom is just starting
With colours to unfold

Peace of mind you'll surely find
Just sitting here to gaze
Upon life's simple wonders
To enjoy for all your days

Me x

(On a friend's farm)

Tripping Round Australia

You're off on an adventure
To visit places you've not seen
You'll have so many memories then
Of the places you have been

We wish you luck in all you do
So just enjoy your time
And make the most of everything
We hope it is sublime

Me x

(Nephew and his wife leaving for their Australian Trip)

Saturday Morning Cycle Along the Bay

Saturday morning out for a ride
The waves simply rolling along with the tide
People out walking their dogs on the beach
A Collie chasing gulls – just out of reach

The clouds seem so huge just floating above
Gentle breeze on my face, soft as a dove
A wonderful feeling of peace can be found
As I cycle on – nature's wonders around

The flowers are opening as they see the sun
A beautiful morning has just begun
There are many pleasures down by the sea
And these are to treasure, if you take time to see

Your thoughts just go back to memories of old
As you cycle passed, swaying flowers of gold
A childhood moment comes to mind
This is so wonderful – not left behind

You look at the people walking by

You give a smile, or just say "Hi"

These simple pleasures just riding along

Too precious to miss, before each moment is gone

Me x

Sunday Morning Swing

Sitting here on my patio
In the early morning light
The trees are swaying gently
After a very pleasant night

My truly lovely family
Still sleeping the time away
I am looking at the deep blue sea
We're in for a very hot day

The sound of sprinklers just nearby
Watering the gardens well
Seagulls flying all around
Breakfasts cooking, a lovely smell

Only a few clouds, here and there
The sky is a lovely blue
Flowers are opening slowly
They all add to the wonderful view

The trees are swaying a wee bit more
A cycle is not to be
I am picturing all these natural things
As I look out to sea

It gives me so much pleasure
Just to sit here on my swing
And take in all the lovely sights
- Nature is a wonderful thing

Me x

Along the Bay

Walking along the sandy beach
Many footprints do abound
From the sunny day we had before
Broken sandcastles, big holes can be found

Oh what pleasures can be had
On the lovely changing sand
The waves just lapping on the shore
Families walking hand in hand

The sound of the sea as waves roll in
So relaxing for the mind
Birds are diving further out
In the deep, for fish they hope to find

A fisherman throwing out his line
As far as he can just from the beach
With a pelican hovering by his side
The fish just out of its reach

The sun is shining way up high
And makes us feel just fine
To think that all these wonderful sights
Are so precious and all mine

Me x

Flying High over Warnbro Sound

Flying high in the light blue sky
Must be a feeling, second to none
Following each other and acrobats too
In the warmth of the midday sun

I can only imagine how it must be
Like a bird with an outstretched wing
Circling around, flying up, flying down
Not thinking of an unpleasant thing

Your cares disappear, just the job in hand
Of flying the plane over sea and land
Looking at life with a bird's eye view
As I sit on my patio, gazing at you

The pleasures you bring to my friends and I
As we gaze up and see, two planes in the sky
Entertainment you've brought, unbeknown to you
Over the years, I would like to thank you

Me x

(Small 'planes over the bay)

Sunday Morn on the Patio

Sitting here on this peaceful morn
Just a few hours, after dawn
The sea, so calm, boats passing by
So many things seen with the naked eye

'Planes flying high in skies white and blue
Jet bikes pulling skiers through
Waters so still, of blue and green
So many wonders to be seen

Life is so pleasant
You think "Why can't it be"
Like this through the world
Living in peace and harmony

I don't suppose it will ever be
A world without fighting and pain
So in your own heart, just let it be
That love and peace always reign

Me x

My Best Friend

To my very "bestest" friend I send
Birthday wishes from the heart
There may be miles between us
But - no distance in our heart

I wish I could be with you
To celebrate in style
But my love is being sent your way
- Our visit - will wait a while

Thank you for your friendship
I treasure it always
With many happy times we've spent
- So many lovely days

I hope today will be special
Just as you are to me
So accept my birthday wishes
From just across the sea

Me

x

Sisters' Saturday Morning Cycle

Another Saturday morning
Out for a ride
Along the sea's pathway
A bluey-green tide

I dreamt of this moment
Another perfect day
And my Sister with me
On holiday, from the UK

We cycle along
Without a real care
Taking in sights
Of everything there

There are boats being moored
Which wait for a while
Until there's a space
When they take off in style

Out for the day
Fishermen at the wheel
To see what they catch
For their midday meal

The cray boats returning
From their early morning start
To load up the lorries
Which quickly depart

The pelicans fly in
Low from their flight
And glide over the water
To get a fresh bite

People out walking
Enjoying their day
Other people on bicycles
Riding the opposite way

As we stop to take photos
A man cycling along
A dog in his basket
- With sunglasses on!

An elderly couple
In their electric car
Driving by the sea shore
- How happy they are

Such wonderful moments
Such great memories
As we cycle the shore
Of the blue and green seas
Me x

(Sister on holiday from UK)

The Garden of Love

Sitting in the bleak morning air
Cat by my side, I sit and stare
At the rain falling, cold, but yet
The plants are grateful, all dripping wet

It's lovely to see clouds drifting by
As I look up at the grey-blue sky
Not the sun – on this Friday morn
Just the fine evergreen, with raindrops adorn

Little ornaments are seen here and there
As I sit in wonder, on my broken chair
To see life grow from a small root
This wonderful garden, from love did shoot

Tender hands made this garden grow
With love and compassion, it really does show
Hard work is the key to toil the ground
But the true feeling is, love does abound

The feeling has passed
The darkness has gone
Between the clouds
A glimpse of the sun

The raindrops are falling
But just from the leaves
A glittering spider web
Is seen through the trees

The birds are now chirping
The sun has come out
In just a few hours
A real turn about

The sound of the traffic
The drips of the rain
The shadows are cast
From the sunshine again

The birds are just flying
From one bush to another
Looking for breakfast
- Some feast to discover

Another day dawns
To enjoy while we may
There are so many wonders
To be seen in a day

Me x

(Early morning in a friend's garden)

Our Lovely Pam

Pam had no brothers and sisters
That we know was true
But she was **so** very blessed
With loving family and friends too

Pam was so very special
To us all in every way
Living life just to the full
Thinking of others every day

For me, I flew many miles away
To live across the sea
But in all the years we'd been apart
Pam was always there for me

We'd alternate each month and ring
To chat about – just everything
But always making sure that we
Were all ok, either side of the sea

Pam has a wonderful family
Who I know was so proud of
Always being there for her
Together, filling their home with love

I know we'll miss our lovely Pam
But in our hearts she'll always stay
As someone so very special
Will be with us forever and a day

Me x

(I wrote and read poem for Cousin Pam at her funeral in the UK)

Naburn Farm

Sitting on the veranda high
Hills and mountains reach the sky
The trees all standing, tall and still
On the side of the winding hill

Cows are munching, slow and calm
In the paddocks on the farm
Horses grazing among the trees
Now branches swaying in the breeze

It is so peaceful sitting here
Gazing across the paddocks near
Birds are chirping high above
And dogs just lazing in this place of love

Me x

(On a friend's farm)

Walking and Reminiscing

Up and out early
On my morning walk
No friend with me
With whom to talk

My thoughts just wander
Here and there
Watching the ocean
Without a care

So many seagulls
Flying all around
Other flocks sitting
On the ground

Are they nesting?
Looks like it to me
But no – only huddled
Together by the sea

Life seems so simple
Just walking along
Then reality hits you
Like a big gong

The pain I am feeling
Just won't go away
I am trying to get through
Each and every day

My Brother has joined
Our family in the sky
I look for reasons
And always ask "Why?"

It just seems too early
To be taken above
He'll perhaps never know
Of how much love

We all felt for him
He was so special it's true
So thoughtful, so caring
In all he would do

My tears are just falling
As I sit by the sea
I just can't explain
How much he meant to me

To be there from the start
Of his journey through life
To share so many years
Through to his children and wife

The years spent together
So many happy times
Looking after him
Reading him many rhymes

The bond that just grew
Between us, so strong
And when he got older
He'd always come along

We'd play in the garden
Be splashing in the pool
And with all the family
Play snooker n' darts – so cool

Always good at "numbers"
And from the age of four
He'd take the numbers of the darts
Adding them to make the score!

When he was eight
Piano lessons he had
I would take him each week
It really was not a fad!

After years of lessons
It became so clear
How proficient he was
Passing exams every year

Beautiful music he'd play
Second to none
- All composers he'd try
But Chopin was the one

He loved many sports
And at the top of his list
Football, playing or watching
And games – he never missed

- At the beginning
When playing for school
He would just stand there
And wait for the ball !!

But, as he got older
The interest was stronger
He'd get stuck right in
"Ball waiting" – no longer

Tennis and squash
He'd play in later years
Often meeting after work
Challenging his peers

We all spent so many years
On holiday and at home
With us four, Mum, Dad and Fossie
Before going off to roam

He loved Mum and Dad so much
Looking after them so well
And even when he left home
His love and caring never fell

His work was so important
Becoming a big part of his life
Dealing with many queries
Avoiding too much strife

He loved solving problems
With results that would be great
Perhaps this was, just too much
And would be part of his fate

Visits to and from Australia
We made in later years
Spending many precious times
With laughter and some tears

There are so many memories
Too numerous to explain
But these are deep within my heart
And always will remain

To love someone so deeply
And lose him in his early years
Brings deep pain and heartache
And so many heartfelt tears

But, looking over his full life
- Pleasures he brought to one another
No wonder, to me, he'll always be
- A wonderful, special Brother

Luv always
Me x

(For my special brother, nicknamed Fossie)

A Dear Friend

Emilé was so special
To us in every way
She was just a trouper
Each and every day

She always was so pleasant
And could tell a tale or two
Making people really laugh
If they were feeling blue

She would always think of others
And be there if she could
Helping out in any way
And always for the good

She was so adventurous
And would fly across the sea
To paint, or cook or holiday
With friends and family

Walking on the beach each day
Whether morning or early night
Her mind may even wander off
To a place just out of sight

She loved the simple things of life
Flowers, birds, dolphins in the sea
Watching from her kitchen window
Inviting friends passing by, for tea

And even through her recent pain
She would always give us time
With all her very thoughtful ways
She was a dear friend of mine

She loved her family oh so much
And was as proud as she could be
Treasuring all the wonderful years
As the family grew, just like a tree

I know Emilé will be sadly missed
But will never be apart
From her loving friends and family
As she'll stay deep within our heart

Me x

(Written on the passing of a dear friend)

May Storm

The storm is coming
White caps on the sea
The clouds look angry
As they sail by me

The trees are bending
Down to the floor
As I sit here wondering
"Now what is in store?"

The newscaster reads –
"Batten everything down"
As hurricane winds
Are expected in town

No boats can be seen
On the horizon today
Because of bad weather
They're all moored in the bay

Not too many people
Out walking their dogs
I expect many are sleeping
In their beds, just like logs

The storm is a feature
Of the weathers that be
And I see it coming
As I sit by the sea

Me x

My Lovely Sister's Special Birthday

This is a very special day
Your 70th it's true
I hope you have lovely time
And know I'm thinking of you

There may be miles between us
But they cannot keep us apart
As growing up through all these years
Love is deep within our heart

As kids we had such lovely times
Wonderful holidays and yet
Times were hard for all of us
But deep memories have been set

I may have been a nuisance
When the boys were on the scene
And seem to get right in the way
As in charge, you must have been

There may be special memories
Which you keep within a box
But I know a special one
- You loved to have new socks!

There have been such good times
Some sad, that may be true
But with our love for each other
We all seemed to just pull through

And even though, with ups and downs
We came through the other end
And grew even closer
Becoming wonderful friends

Our families are special
And we hold treasured memories true
So on your very special day
I send love from me to you

Love always
Linda xx

(My sister's birthday in the UK)

Star Gazing

Looking up at the midnight sky
Satellites twinkling as they race by
Between the stars all shiny and bright
Just gazing above in the peaceful night

Your mind starts to wander
Many thoughts just pass through
Sometimes they are plans, or
"Just what shall I do?"

If you have a problem
You cannot sort out
It's so good to ponder
And let feelings out

Just laying at night
Under a star filled sky
It's good to let go of things
And let the world go by

Me x

(Just laying on sun bed on patio)

"Calma" The Dolphin

Early on a Friday morn
Whilst walking along the bay
We came upon a gentle man
Trying to "save the day"

A baby dolphin, left alone
It's mother, taken away
With kindness and a lot of love
He cradled her come what may

But try as he might
And with all his care
The struggle for this dolphin
Was just too much to bear

So silently she slipped away
Leaving broken hearts behind
But I hope this baby dolphin
Knew that people had been kind

Me x

(Baby dolphin found alone in the bay)

Farewell to My Lovely Grandsons

To my lovely Grandsons
I would like to say
Thank you for a wonderful time
During your Australian holiday

I have had such a lovely time
Having you here with me
And thank you both for travelling
Far across the sea

The fun we've had, the hide and seek
The walks along the bay
Breakfast time and lunches too
Eating lots each and every day

The sandy beach, sand castles too
And jumping over the waves
In and out of the ocean
On those sunny fun-filled days

The toys upon the patio
I hope that was fun
And the swinging gently
For Luke in the sun

The happy times that we have shared
Will stay with me forever
And hope we'll be together soon
Making more memories to treasure

All my love
Nanny BB xx

(My grandsons returning to the UK after a holiday)

First day of Winter

The first day of winter
Has now arrived
As I watch from the patio
A coloured bird has just dived
Into the Bottle Brush tree, in flower
To see what goodies it can devour

Up and down the branches it flits
As a friend of his, comes and sits
On a different branch to look for food
Thinking this tree is full of all things good

The sea is dark blue
But the sun is shining bright
Through many white clouds
The temperature, just right

It is so pleasant
Sitting here to gaze
At life's simple treasures
On bright sunny days

The evenings are cooler
And darker early too
So I make the most of sunny days
And simply enjoy the view

Me x

From my Patio

Round in a circle
The pelicans fly
Up in the clouds
Soaring so high

The sea is so calm
They are watching well
To look for their fodder
Before the big swell

They are so graceful
And follow so true
One after the other
Through skies, white and blue

It is so peaceful
Just sitting here
Watching as nature
Surrounds me so near

No cars driving through
And making a noise
- Not even children
Playing with their toys

It is so pleasant
Watching boats sailing by
Being the objects
In a pelican's eye

The white and blue clouds
Being met by some grey
Perhaps there'll be rain
Later in the day

But just for now
I am enjoying this day
Watching birds diving
O'er the sea for their prey

The sun has come out
And no breeze in sight
I think I'll just sit here
'Till day turns to night !!

Me x

Farewell to My Lovely Grandchildren

Archie and Leah the time has come
To say farewell it's true
But I hope you have a lovely time
Looking forward to all things new

I will miss you very much
And have enjoyed looking after you
While Mum and Dad went out to work
The special things that we would do

Writing, reading, making cards and cooking too
All of the lovely things just with you
Down on the beach, in and out of the waves
These were truly memorable days

The nights on the patio
Looking up at the stars
Searching for a *shopping trolley*
Oh – there's the moon – where is Mars?

I hope you'll remember these times too
As I really enjoyed just being with you
Such precious times to keep in my memory
Which I will treasure in my heart eternally
All my love Nanny xx
(My grandchildren returning to the UK after 2 years)

J C's Birthday 2014

Oh it's another Birthday
That you could be here with me
I have just strolled along the beach
Paddling in the warm blue sea

I have such lovely memories
Of the years we spent together
And I know they'll never fade
They will stay with me forever

I think of all the happy times
We could have spent with our family
All being together and now
With a larger family tree

You would have loved to spend your time
With your grandchildren by your side
Running along the beach or even
On your bikes, going for a ride

I am sorry that you left us
When you did, just in your prime
But I treasure all our happy years
And so glad that you were mine
Love always
x Linzee x

Mother's Day

Today is so emotional
But the sun is shining bright
The sky is blue and lovely
And the fluffy clouds, so white

A small 'plane is putting on a show
Flying high into the blue
Then twirling round as it comes down
Oh what a wonderful view

The telephone keeps ringing
With offers to take me out
To celebrate this special day
It's lovely having friends about

But my thoughts are with my family
So far across the sea
And I just can't help thinking
I wish they were here with me

I know they have their lives to live
And do things as they may
But wish we were together
On this special 'Mother's Day'

But the love I hold dear in my heart
Will help me through the day
And bring us close together
Although we are miles away

I treasure all our memories
Of Mother's Days gone by
Spending many happy hours
My lovely family and I

Me x

(Mother's Day 2014)

About the Author

I was very happy as a child, at home with Mum, Dad and my three siblings. I loved reading and visited the local library regularly for many years. I also started reading poetry and remember being given a little red suede bound poetry book, which I treasured and read from time to time.

At the age of ten, we were all blessed with another wonderful brother, growing up together for a while, until all three elder siblings married and left home. We were all very close and our family had treasured memories full of love and togetherness.

Years went by and I did not read so much, but when I learnt shorthand at school, I found it a lot easier and quicker, to write down my feelings, translating and writing in longhand or typing, after. My poetry writing had started.

Over my life I have wonderful memories of my own family and my Mother's too, of all the lovely times spent together, but there are also the sad times and I just seemed to take in all the emotions of the day, putting my feelings to verse. I feel love and caring give strength to help people get through many unpleasant times.

I met John (J C) and we married, went overseas to experience other parts of the world, started our family with a gorgeous son, then returned to England, completing our family, with a beautiful daughter.

After years back in England, we all immigrated to Australia, but unfortunately JC died after 6 months of a heart attack. Our love for each other kept us going, although a difficult time.

Eventually our children returned to UK after living between there and Australia, both having settled with their families in the UK.

Testimonials

"Linda's poetry captures moments in time with amazing sentiment, and heartfelt thoughts. The snapshot of a particular event or happening, both sad and joyful, is put down in words for us all to enjoy."

Glenn

"The deepest most selfless heart full of nothing but love. Truly one of nature's kindest creations. Love you xx"

Dina

"For those of us who know Linda very well, we know she does everything 'From the Heart'. When you read the words in this book you will know she not only writes 'From the Heart' but from her very soul."

Tania

www.ingramcontent.com/pod-product-compliance
Lightning Source LLC
Chambersburg PA
CBHW042051290426
44110CB00001B/19